Good Swastika, Bad Swastika

An Example of the Importance
of Spatial Directions

Jonathan D. Worcester

Good Swastika, Bad Swastika
An Example of the Importance of Spacial Directions

Copyright © 2024 Jonathan D. Worcester
Fairfield, Iowa U.S.A.

All Rights reserved. No part of this publication may be reproduced, stored in a retrieval system, or transmitted in any form or by any means, electronic, mechanical, photocopying, recording, or otherwise, without permission in writing from the author.

Printed in the United States of America

Cover and book design by the author.
Typeset in Noto Sans, and Noto Serif TC
Text formatted in Pages.

ISBN 9781977791672

Other books by Jonathan Worcester:

The Scales of Heaven and Earth; The Tonal Basis of the Ancient Music of India (2016)

Lao Tsu on the Actions of the Highest Rulers; Understanding Chapter 17 of the Tao Te Ching (2016)

Fundamental Patterns and Functions of Consciousness (2024)

Pronunciation of Sanskrit Words:

A number of Sanskrit words occur in the text. I use the standard Roman character set which allows for proper pronunciation.

The website https://learnsanskrit.org/guide/core/ gives instructions for pronunciation of all the characters used. The first seven core lessons cover all of the Sanskrit sounds, their articulation points, and the corresponding letters.

Dedicated to those

who desire self-knowledge,

the comprehensive betterment

of themselves and society,

and the highest good for all

Table of Contents

Introduction	1
The Vedic Directions and their Qualities	4
The Left-Facing "ideal" Swastika	15
The Right-Facing "Capitalistic" Swastika	21
The Less-Good Swastikas	26
The Left-Facing 45° Rotated "Nomadic" Swastika	27
The Right-Facing 45° Rotated "Egotistic" Swastika	33
A Closer Analysis of the Eight Directions	39
Concluding Remarks	42
References and Notes	46

Introduction

This Swastika:

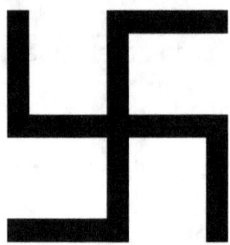

is revered in India, Tibet, and China as a symbol of good fortune. It is found in Hindu temples, in Chinese decorative designs, and is part of the official character set for the Tibetan language. [1] I was surprised to find it on maps as a symbol for Buddhist temples when I was a student in Japan.

Su means *good, righteous, virtuous*. *Asti* means *is*. *Swastika* then denotes a state of being good or righteous. Most scholars consider it to be a symbol of the all-beneficent sun moving across the sky. What can be more auspicious than the sun in a clear blue sky on a good day?

Good Swastika, Bad Swastika

This Swastika:

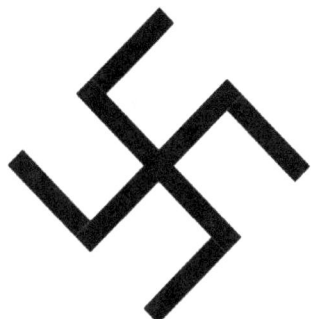

evokes fear and fearful memories in the Western world and is the symbol that is brought to mind when the word *Swastika* is thought or heard there.

Most people know that it was the insignia of the Nazi Party in Germany and of the Nazi regime when that party came to power, rising out of the chaos of economic collapse after World War I. It signifies the promotion of racial and cultural superiority, hatred, militarism, the appropriation of goods and lands, and the confinement and extermination of unwanted people and groups (notably Jews, Gypsies, minority religious groups, invalids, and the mentally feeble).

The first swastika was also used sometimes by the Nazis, but this one had prominent use, being found on the ubiquitous flags and armbands.

Introduction

There are some people and groups who use this swastika today to proclaim that they wish to emulate the actions of the Nazis in society.

It seems it could be correct to call the first a *good swastika* and the second a *bad swastika*, at least based on the commonly held morality of the major religions.

There is another level of analysis which will be applied in this book. It uses deeper symbolic meanings based on the qualities given to the directions in the Vedic tradition of India. Orientation in space turns out to mean a lot, and the meanings turn out to be consistent with the good and bad posited here.

There are two other swastikas, with their arms turning left, rather than right, which will also be considered.

The starting point is the qualities of the directions.

Good Swastika, Bad Swastika

The Vedic Directions and their Qualities

The Vedic tradition considers that the eight main directions on the horizon are presided over by deities. These deities are called the *Lokapālas* (*Guardians of the Directions* — literally, *of the places*). Another term for them is *Dig Devatās* (*Deities of the Directions*). [2]

As each deity is understood to have particular qualities and purposes in creation, the directions can be thought to have the same characteristics.

The analysis will start with the deities, explore their qualities, then use those qualities for analyzing the four swastikas.

Also considered is how the end points of each swastika's arm can be seen as the result of adding the qualities of its two segments in sequence. The symbolic meaning of the four arms of each swastika is therefore unique — the meanings of each arm are not replicated in any other swastika.

With this preparation, it will be easy to make clear decisions about the nature of each of a swastika's four arms, and of each swastika as a whole.

The Vedic Directions and their Qualities

The Vedic Deities (*Devatās*)

In the morning, the sun comes up in the east. This is how one orients oneself. The meaning of the word o*rient* is *the eastern direction*. From this orientation, one also knows the other directions. In the the diagrams, east will be at the top, as if one faces east looking out at what is there.

East

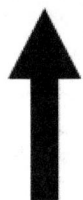

In the Vedic understanding, who is responsible for the eastern direction? It is *Indra*, king of the *Devatās*.

What does a good king do? He administers his realm, seeing that everyone gets what is needed to live and work well and restraining everyone from taking what belongs to others. He is the prime coordinating intelligence of the realm.

East relates to mind, administration, and co-ordination.

In the opposite direction is west.

West

In the Vedic understanding, who is in charge here? It is *Varuṇa*, Lord of Water.

Water is the a primary constituent of the life of the body. All physiological processes require it. Nourishment is carried in it. Growth and generation use this fluid medium. It is also an important means of communication, carrying hormones to regulate cellular and glandular activity.

West is physical connection, generation, and nourishment.

The Vedic Directions and their Qualities

North is the direction going left.

In the Vedic understanding, *Kubera*, the Lord of Wealth, rules north.

This direction is concerned with the perception of value, everything and everyone being seen for the unique values they contain.

North is the perception of value.

Good Swastika, Bad Swastika

South is the direction to the right.

 **South**

In the Vedic understanding, *Yama*, the Lord of Death, rules the south. *Yama* is also *Dharma Raj*, the Lord of Natural Law, the evolutionary direction for everybody and everything in creation. Every action has an effect. *Yama* discriminates each action and sees that every action has its proper consequences. It may be that the final consequence of life is death, but many more effects come before that final one. The discriminating function of *Yama* can be seen as the intellect. In general, the knowledge of cause and effect is the basis for making laws.

South is intellect, which involves perception of qualities and discernment of cause and effect. It also represents laws, both universal and manmade.

The Vedic Directions and their Qualities

These four directions are all one needs to construct the *good* swastika shown at the beginning. But the start and end points also need to be understood.

The Point at the Center

The beginning point at the center of each swastika represents the full potential of life. I deduce this because, in the Vedic understanding, *Brahma*, the Creator, stands above, and *Viṣṇu*, the Sustainer stands below. [3] *Brahma* creates from the unmanifest potential within *Viṣṇu*. It is the interaction between the two that creates life and gives it its dynamism. That potential flows into the functions represented by the four outgoing arm segments, then flows along the segments on the edges to the four end points.

The central point is the full potential of life.

The Intermediate Points

These are the four intermediate directions and represent in this analysis four other basic functions in creation.

Southeast is associated with ***Agni***, **Fire**, whose nature is **specific, transformational change**. The first thought might be that fire destroys what it burns. While it is true that the structure of the fuel is destroyed, the atoms involved do not change. The destruction is the result of many *specific changes* in the configuration of the fuel molecules as they combine with oxygen in the air. Each change is specific, resulting in a state that is less energetic, the exact energy difference between the states being radiated off as heat or light.

Northwest is associated with ***Vāyu***, **Air (Wind)** whose nature is **spontaneous flow** and **locational change**.

Southwest is associated with ***Nirṛti***, **Lord of Decay** and conceivably of **Order**. *Nir* can mean both *not* and *completely*. *Ṛiti* means *order*. Thus *Nirṛiti* can relate both to disorder and order. *Nirṛiti* presides over the anus, where what is not assimilated from the food eaten is removed from life processes as an inert substance. Any creation of structure in the body involves a similar process (separation, removal, structure). **Earth element**, **structure**, and **purification** belong here.

Northeast is associated with ***Īśānas*** who relates to ***being***, **silent contentment**, and, in this context, also **storehouse of impressions** and **memory**. Memories and resting contentment are the locus of **ego**.

The Vedic Directions and their Qualities

In brief:

> Southeast: Specific, Transformational Change
>
> Northwest: Locational Change
>
> Southwest: Structure and Purification
>
> Northeast: Ego and Storehouse of Impressions

Now to consider the different paths from the center to the end points.

Any leg of a swastika arm in the same direction can be thought to embody the same qualities. That being so, it still matters where that leg started.

For instance, all legs going east represent coordination. If the leg starts from the center, it imbibes full potential for its coordinating processes. It is unimpeded by any other functions. If it starts along the periphery, say after the northern evaluative function, it can only administer the value that prior function has generated. It does what it can to deliver a balanced result to the Ego in the Northeast corner from the value it has received.

Therefore, the legs from the center will be called *primary*. The legs that go at right angles from the primary legs will be be called *secondary*.

Good Swastika, Bad Swastika

The map below gives an illustration of this. It shows two business trips starting in Zagreb, Croatia's capitol, and ending in Amsterdam.

On this trip goods are purchased along the way to be sold in Amsterdam. The purchases will be made only when going north. Going west, there will be no purchases, but the merchant will be accompanied by a person with great knowledge of the markets in Amsterdam and of the sellers along the route who have the best goods to purchase.

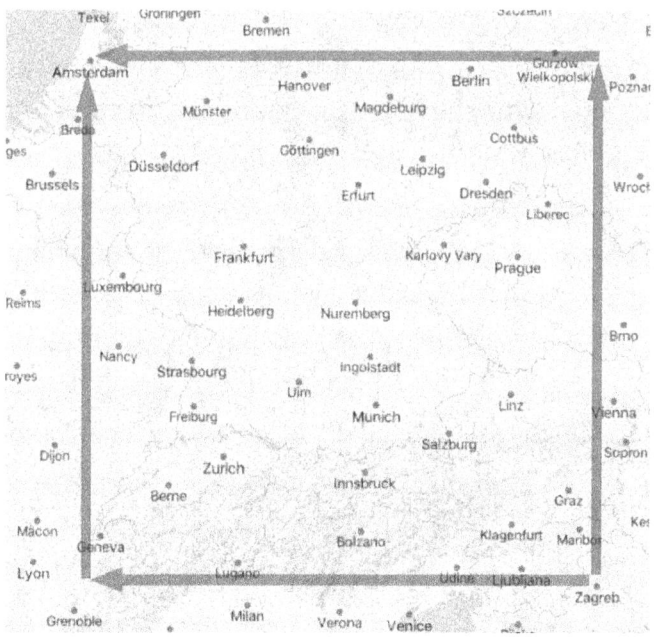

© OpenStreetMap contributors

The Vedic Directions and their Qualities

For journey one, the merchant goes west first: traveling with the expert through southern Slovenia, northern Italy, and Switzerland, entering France; then turning north to make purchases, entering and traversing Belgium and arriving in the Netherlands from the south.

For journey two, the merchant goes north first, making purchases: traveling through western Slovenia, Austria, Czechia, and Poland; then turning west, joined by the expert, entering and traversing Germany and entering the Netherlands from the east.

Considering the two itineraries, the merchant will likely purchase better goods for sale and get a better return if the merchant starts by going west.

On journey One, while going west, the merchant plans with the expert what to purchase and where to sell. Then, while going north, the merchant purchases the best possible goods; at length, selling these to the best known buyers in Amsterdam.

On Journey Two, while going north, the merchant purchases goods on the merchant's own, as best as the merchant can. Then, while going west, the expert helps the merchant determine where to sell these goods in Amsterdam. If the merchant is lucky, what the merchant bought will bring a good return. But the expert's recommendations will be limited by what the merchant has already procured.

This illustrates why the sequence of the segments of a swastika's arms makes a difference.

With this preparation, the analysis of the different swastikas for their qualities can begin.

The Left-Facing "ideal" Swastika

Although the Right-Facing Swastika was shown at the beginning of the introduction, the Left-Facing Swastika turns out to have the most beneficial symbolic meanings. So the investigation will start with it.

The eastern arm starts east and turns north, ending in ego with its storehouse of impressions.

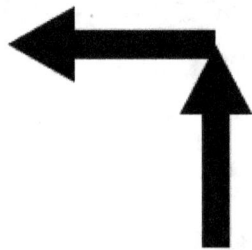

It embodies coordination (east) delivering the values (north) in the situations it administers. These are lodged in the storehouse of impressions, the ego (northeast).

The coordinator is primary; wealth and valuation is secondary.

Since coordination is primary, its product is balanced and maximally realistic. The resultant value of the eastern vector is delivered north to be stored in the ego as a memory. Since this memory has a balanced value, it will not be a source of craving for a new experience in a similar situation. This leaves the person more free for creative action in the future. The Sanskrit word for this freedom is *Mokṣa*, one of the four ends of life [4] in the Vedic understanding.

The Left-Facing "ideal" Swastika

The southern arm starts south and turns east, ending in specific transformations.

It embodies knowledge of cause and effect and natural law (south) which is then administered in a balanced way (east) to create specific changes (southeast)

Knowledge of cause and effect is primary; coordination is secondary.

Here, realistically coordinated transformations in life are regulated according to natural law. Mistakes are minimum or nonexistent. Changes promote real growth which has a holistic value. The Sanskrit word for this is *Dharma*, another of the four aims of life in the Vedic understanding. This process of attuning with natural law is *Yajña*, which is one of the three holy actions [5] in the Vedic understanding.

Good Swastika, Bad Swastika

The western arm starts west and turns south, ending in structure and purification.

It embodies nourishment and physical connection (west) being delivered by the proper discrimination of cause and effect (south), to create a healthy and pure structure of life, either in the body, or in the material environment (southwest).

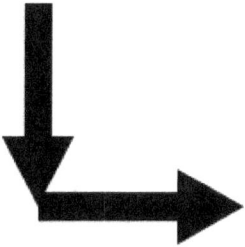

Nourishment and connection is primary; knowledge of cause and effect is secondary.

The joy prevalent in these pure structures is called *Kāma*, another of the four aims of life in the Vedic understanding. The building of orderliness and purity in this process is *tapas* (austerity), another of the three holy actions in the Vedic systems of knowledge. The *Yoga Sūtra* (II.43) states that the result of *tapas* is the destruction of impurities and the perfection of the body and senses. This is a validation of the interpretation presented here.

The Left-Facing "ideal" Swastika

The northern arm starts north and turns west, ending in locational change.

Values gained (north) are used to nourish and connect (west) fostering locational change (northwest).

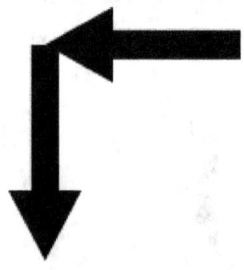

Perception of value (north) is primary; nourishment and physical connection (west) is secondary.

This arm represents movement of nourishing values throughout the environment. This expresses the true purpose of *Artha* (wealth), one of the four aims of life in the Vedic understanding. Because the wealth is flowing out to others, this arm also expresses *Danam* (gift), the third of the holy actions in the Vedic understanding.

Good Swastika, Bad Swastika

The Left-Facing Swastika is maximally beneficial.

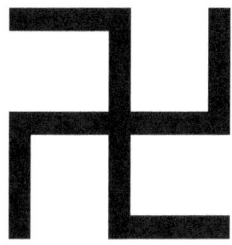

- Properly organized memories are created which will be a basis for balanced, useful actions in the future.
- Transformations are expressions of evaluations of cause and effect and controlled in a balanced way for a holistic outcome.
- Nourishment and pleasure result in health and orderliness through the application of the perception of cause and effect.
- Values obtained are used to nourish people and the surroundings.

This swastika symbolizes the fulfillment of the four aims of life and the three holy actions in the Vedic understanding.

The Right-Facing "Capitalistic" Swastika

The eastern arm starts east and turns south, ending in transformations.

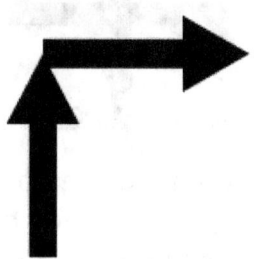

It embodies coordination (east) using knowledge of cause and effect (south) in the situations it administers to create transformations (southeast).

The coordinator is primary; knowledge of cause and effect is secondary.

Transformations are directed by the perceiver of cause and effect according to the administrator's understanding of what should be done. The administrator cannot see everything, but is geared towards change. This gives a quality of constant transformation and intended progress with possible unknown side effects.

The southern arm starts south and turns west, ending in structure and purification.

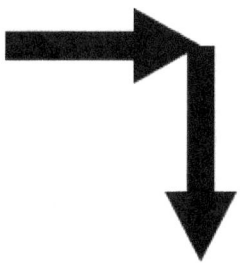

Knowledge of Natural Law — or law in general — (south) is directed to nourishment and physical connections (west), ending in structure and purification (southwest).

Realistic lawfulness is primary; nourishment and physical connections is secondary.

Maintaining the outer, the physical, is a priority for laws and rules. These are usually based on sound logic. The nourishment of the physical is attempted by the application of law.

The Right-Facing "Capitalistic" Swastika

The western arm starts west and turns north, ending in locational change.

Useful goods and services (west) are produced which are judged for value (north) and moved to other locations (northwest).

Nourishment and physical connections are primary; perception of value is secondary.

This is exemplified in industry and commerce. Primary nourishment is not directed towards purity and structure, but towards sales to others.

Good Swastika, Bad Swastika

The northern arm starts north and turns east, ending in the ego.

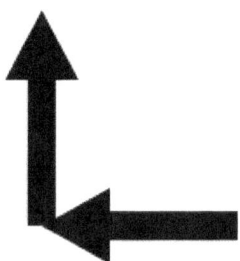

Evaluation of people, objects, and situations (north) is organized and coordinated (east) for the benefit of the ego (northeast).

Perception of value is primary; coordination is secondary.

Individuals are are meant to benefit from the values they find.

The Right-Facing "Capitalistic" Swastika

Putting these four arms together results in a generally auspicious swastika, though symbolically it has some drawbacks.

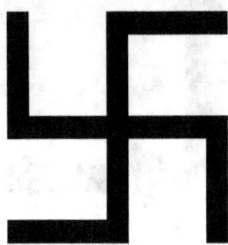

- There is promotion of change and technological progress, though with unseen consequences.
- Laws primarily foster the orderliness of the physical world.
- Goods for the nourishment of people and society are evaluated, then moved into trade and commerce.
- The individual is acknowledged as the primary recipient of values created.

This seems to represent a capitalistic society.

Good Swastika, Bad Swastika

The Less-Good Swastikas

The other two swastikas have an axis that is at 45° from the swastikas just considered. This means that the corners in the intermediate directions (southeast, southwest, northwest, northeast) are connected to the center, and symbolically gain the potential coming from that unbounded source. They then distribute the result to the points in the cardinal directions.

In Vedic cosmology, there is recounted an ascendence either of the *Devas*, the celestials responsible for order, balance, and harmony, or the *Asuras*, the celestials more interested in personal power, enjoyment, and prestige at the expense of overall harmony. Sometimes the *Devas* are occupying their natural place in heaven. Sometimes the *Asuras* invade heaven, expel the *Devas*, and rule the universe as they see fit.

Heaven might be considered the central point of the swastikas. Its rulership might be symbolically represented as having direct access to that center. The other two swastikas might be thought of as representing conditions when the *Asuras* are in charge.

The Left-Facing 45° Rotated "Nomadic" Swastika

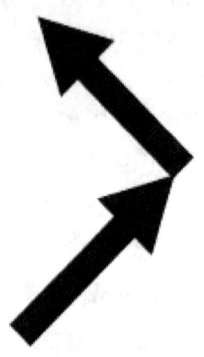

The southeast arm begins to the southeast, then turns to the northeast, ending in co-ordination.

Opportunism within immediate situations (southeast) for the benefit of the ego (northeast) characterize the coordination of activities (east).

Transformative change (southeast) is primary; ego and memory (northeast) is secondary.

Clever, expedient changes for the sake of the ego are basic to the administration of each situation.

The southwest arm begins to the southwest, then turns southeast, ending in perception of cause and effect.

The maintenance of integrity and purity (southwest) drives all specific changes (southeast). This is the basic template for all laws (south).

Structure and purification (southwest) is primary; transformational change (southeast) is secondary.

Laws are formed to maintain the purity and integrity of the social group and are applied according to expediency. They are not based on universal principles, but are created for specific situational needs.

The Left-Facing 45° Rotated "Nomadic" Swastika

The northeast arm begins to the northeast; then turns northwest, ending in valuation (north).

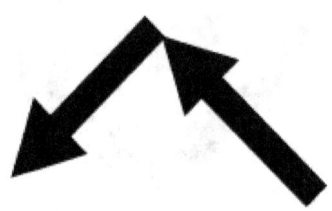

What is owned and known by the ego (northeast), moves through location and location (northwest) and is what is valued (north).

Ego and memory (northeast) are primary; locational change (northwest) is secondary.

Things of value that are appropriated are mainly those characterized by what can be moved easily. Other things of value that are gained are traded for transportable items or otherwise disposed of. Accumulated experience and memories are also highly valued, since, wherever one is, these are available to be used.

The northwest arm begins to the northwest, then turns southwest, ending in nourishment and physical connection.

Change of location (northwest) for the sake of structure and purity (southwest) is the means of nourishment (west)

Locational change (northwest) is primary; structure and purity (southwest) is secondary.

What nourishes life and builds life's structure is movement from place to place with a view to attending to personal conditions.

The Left-Facing 45° Rotated "Nomadic" Swastika

Putting these four arms together results in a swastika that has a mixed value, one reflective of a nomadic life.

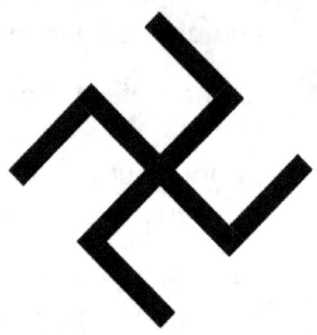

- Clever, resourceful changes based on immediate circumstances and made for the sake of oneself characterize the general administration of life.
- Laws are formed for the benefit of the social group and applied according to expediency. A nomadic band has its own laws and rules that are creatively applied to the lands and societies it moves through.
- Objects are valued that can easily be taken from place to place. Trading less transportable items is common. Memories from past experiences are also highly valued.
- Nourishment (livelihood) comes from movement from location to location.

Good Swastika, Bad Swastika

These characteristics are appropriate for those with a nomadic life. This is a *good* swastika for them.

However, the more settled peoples that the nomads move through may have concerns in dealing with them. The nomads have their own laws and morality. They are clever and ready to take advantage of the situations they find themselves in — a requirement for their livelihood. They are here today and gone tomorrow, so it may not seem appropriate to trust them. From this perspective it is a *bad* swastika, but one which has its reason for being.

The Right-Facing 45° Rotated "Egotistic" Swastika

The southeastern arm begins to the southeast, then turns southwest, ending in knowledge of action and consequence — the value of law (south).

Changes are made according to each situation (southeast), and conform to requirements for purity and structure (southwest). This is the underlying basis for all laws (south).

Transformational change (southeast) is primary; purification and structure (southwest) are secondary.

Laws reflect, not universal principles, but situational expediency directed towards the purity of culture and the physical environment.

The southwestern arm begins to the southwest, then turns northwest, ending in nourishment and connection.

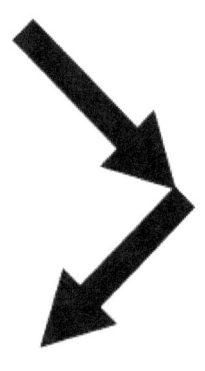

Order and purity (southwest) is attempted by removing unwanted elements (northwest) in hopes of creating a situation of nourishment (west).

Order and purification (southwest) is primary; locational change (northwest) is secondary.

This is a philosophy of nourishment through purification. It excludes the idea of nourishing through nutriments. In terms of a cultural area, the process involves relocating, deporting, or otherwise removing people and unwanted elements, censoring communications to meet strict standards, and, in the extreme, ethnic cleansing — the systematic killing of members of unwanted groups.

The Right-Facing 45° Rotated "Egotistic" Swastika

The northwestern arm begins to the northwest, then turns northeast. ending in values.

Materials move from where they are (northwest) and are appropriated by the ego (northeast) to be enjoyed as value (north).

Locational change (northwest) is primary; self and appropriation (northeast) is secondary.

Value is not so much created as it is appropriated by moving things to oneself to own and enjoy.

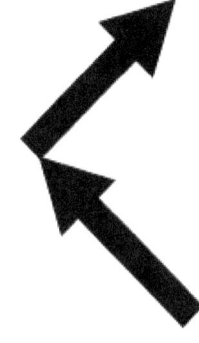

The northeastern arm begins to the northeast, then turns southeast, ending in coordination and administration.

The desires and memories residing in the ego (northeast) stimulate transformations (southeast) for the administration of life (east).

The ego (northeast) is primary; transformative change (southeast) is secondary.

The pragmatic, balanced administration of society, and life in general, is subverted for the sake of administering life according to the ego's set concerns. On a national level, administration is required to be according to a cultural ideal and is applied on a case by case basis.

The Right-Facing 45° Rotated "Egotistic" Swastika

Putting these four arms together results in the least auspicious swastika — what could be called the *bad* swastika.

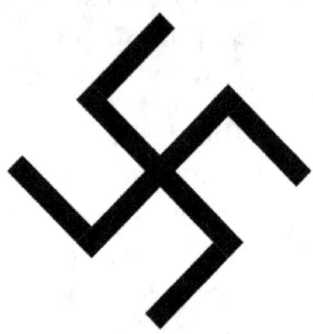

- Transformational changes are made with an aim to increase purity and order. The changes are according to each context (not through recourse to universal principles). The changes become the basis for law. Thus law can be capricious.
- Society is attempted to be nourished by activities to create order and purity. These involve the physical removal of unwanted elements — in the extreme, ethnic cleansing.
- Materials are moved and appropriated for personal use. Value is taken more than is created.
- Administration of society is through transformations initiated for the sake of the ego

and memory of its historical value, as opposed to unbiased empirical coordination.

One would hope that most people would not support the orientation towards the world that this swastika symbolically represents. But the Nazi regime, which had this swastika as its symbol, embodied much of what is found here. And there are people today who, either in desperation or in temperament, believe this is the way to achieve fulfillment.

A Closer Analysis of the Eight Directions

What makes the primary difference between the *good* and the *bad* swastikas?

One consideration is that two separate sets of directions are used in each type. The aligned and rotated swastikas each use a set of four directions. In both cases, each direction is used twice: once as primary from the center; once as secondary along an edge.

The directions used by the aligned swastikas represent *connection and nourishment*; *perception of value*; *coordination*; and *perception of cause and effect*. These together present a pragmatic, balanced outcome.

The directions used by the rotated swastikas are *structure and purification*; *transformational change*; *locational change*; and *ego with its storehouse of impressions*. Two of these involve unregulated change, and two are characterized by activities directed to maintenance of particular values. Balanced progress is unlikely.

A crucial factor, as well, is the position of the ego.

Each direction represents a fundamental function in life. The coordinating mind and the discriminating intellect are tools of one's self. So too are one's appreciation of value, one's processes that nourish and connect, one's ability to make changes in one's surroundings and to make changes of one's location, and one's building of purified structure.

The ego, as a storehouse of memories, is a function which is more than a tool. Memories activated, create one's identity — and this identity becomes one's sense of self.

Ego is the only function that is self-aware [6]. If it becomes primary, as is the case in the 45° rotated swastikas, the whole of life becomes limited and subservient to the individual's or the culture's memory and sense of identity.

The true self is the point at the center. It relates everything to everything in a balanced way, according to each component's nature. Separation from this relation to the wholeness of life distorts these natural relations.

That is why, when Jesus was asked about the essence of holy law, he replied, *"'You shall love the Lord your God with all your heart, with all your soul, and with all your mind.' This is the first and great commandment. And the second is like it: 'You shall love your neighbor as yourself'"* (Matthew 22:37-40, New King James Version). These two

A Closer Analysis of the Eight Directions

commandments are meant to expand the ego to become universal by making it subservient to God and to one's fellows — something that may be hard to do, especially when survival seems threatened.

There is nothing more important to the ego than protection of the ego and the furtherance of its plans. By making the ego a corner of the standard swastikas, ego becomes secondary and gains its power indirectly from the eastern or northern arms. There it performs its important function of being a touchstone that relates new experiences to memories and one's identity and initiates responses — without impeding the balanced operations of other functions of life.

Good Swastika, Bad Swastika

Concluding Remarks

The eight functions considered here are so basic that they exist at a level deeper than thought. They are activated from there according to habit and circumstances. Each swastika portrays all eight as midpoints and corners of the perimeter of a square, and their source as the point at the square's center.

Viewing the swastikas as eight arrows — four from the center and four on the periphery — it becomes clear that there is a certain incompleteness and imbalance to the figures.

Four arrows are missing along the edges, and four more could be added returning from the midpoints to the source at the center. Finally, the total picture involves arrows to both the right and left around the periphery of the square.

The result is the figure on the next page that embodies more completely the dynamics of life. The two *good* swastikas are there, but are hidden in the larger picture.

Concluding Remarks

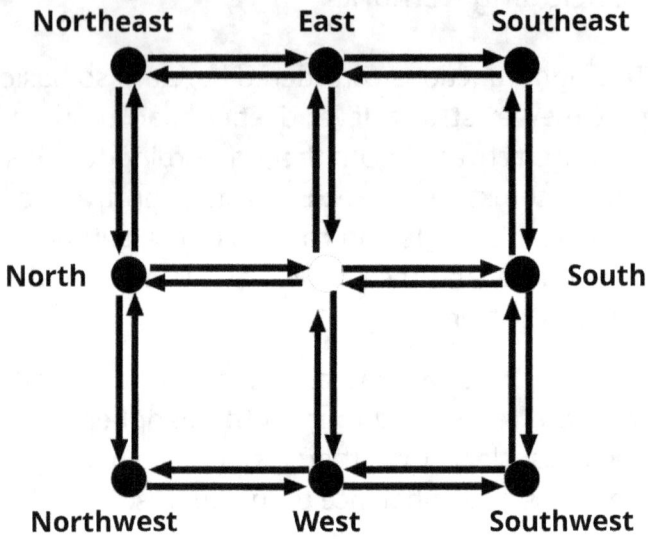

With this, richer and more complex possibilities open up which can extend what was considered so far.

Going further may be more of interest at this point to scholars.

Viewing the rise of nationalism and identity politics in the world, what is presented here has the most immediate usefulness.

If the qualities of the directions as arrayed in the swastikas represent an essential organization of life, the choices made for the operation of society create linked sets of realities that will be lived in life. Particular states of valuation, administration, nourishment, and law go together. A major change in one of these, changes everything. May the choices be for the best.

***

The subtitle of this book refers to the importance of the spatial directions. The question arises: Does looking at swastikas with different orientations really evoke the symbolic sense suggested for each?

The ancient architectural systems of *Sthāpatya Veda* in India and *Feng Shui* [7] in China clearly define qualities for the eight directions and give great importance to proper alignment.

Also, whenever one looks at something, the directions are implicit. If qualities exist in the directions, they will be reflected in any object of sight as well.

More tellingly, in the early decades of the Twentieth Century, the swastika was a popular design element in Europe. The Nazi party chose it as an emblem, believing it to be a symbol associated with the Aryan race.

They could have chosen any spatial orientation. The left-facing swastika was available, with its implicit character of balanced administration,

Concluding Remarks

discernment of value, nourishment, and discrimination of cause and effect, leading to freedom, generosity, well-being, and progressive change — as were the two representing capitalistic and nomadic life.

But they chose, in the main, the right-facing 45° rotated swastika, with the implicit meaning of administration aimed at enforcing national memory, situationally based laws directed to removing and destroying foreign elements, attempts at nourishment through purification and separation, and confiscation of value from others. Some of these were stated goals. All were policies when they came to power. Could their choice have been more than a coincidence?

***

Having extended the ancient Vedic understanding of the directions to the swastikas, the results have been more than might have been imagined. This may be enough for us to take spatial orientation seriously.

References and Notes

Much of the content of this book is based on a chapter on the ten directions in my book *Fundamental Patterns and Functions of Consciousness*. That work is, by nature of the material, more scholarly and abstract. It has fairly complete citations which cover all material except the swastikas themselves, which were not treated there.

[1] Wikipedia has this webpage that relates to my general description of the swastika: https://en.wikipedia.org/wiki/Swastika.

[2] https://en.wikipedia.org/wiki/Guardians_of_the_directions#Lokap%C4%81las is a source for the *Lokapālas*. Details about each of the *Lokapālas* are easily available from Internet searches. Understanding their names from the Sanskrit roots that underlie them requires familiarity with the use of Sanskrit dictionaries. I utilized Monier-Williams Sanskrit Dictionary (https://www.sanskrit-lexicon.uni-koeln.de/scans/MWScan/2020/web/webtc/index-caller.php).

A search on the Internet for "Vastu Purusha" also will bring articles and images giving the directions and associated *Devatās*. Some differences exist for a couple of the directions. In

References and Notes

those cases, I have chosen the *Devatā* most consistent with the overall dynamics implicit in the interactions among the directions.

Through my years of thought on this topic, I have concluded that the *Lokapālas* also can be seen to exemplify the eight primary functions of creation given in the Vedic literature: earth, water, fire, air, space, mind, intellect, and ego. In most cases the relation is straightforward. In the others, a logic presents itself that justifies linking the *Devatā* with a fundamental function.

The choosing of the descriptions of the *Devatās* from their sometimes extensive characteristics and histories and the extrapolations of the qualities for the directions is my own doing. I do not feel that I have done an injustice to the traditional understandings, but I also realize that there is more that can be said.

[3] The story of the *Vastu Purusha* in the Vedic literature gives *Devatās* for up and down. They are *Brahma*, the Creator above, and *Viṣṇu*, the Sustainer below. *Brahma* creates from the unmanifest potential within *Viṣṇu*. It is the interaction between the two that creates life and gives it its dynamism.

Good Swastika, Bad Swastika

[4] See https://en.wikipedia.org/wiki/Puru%E1%B9%A3%C4%81rtha for a discussion of the four aims of life.

[5] The three holy actions, to be continued even after enlightenment is gained, are related by Kṛṣṇa in the *Bhagavad Gītā*, Chapter 18, verse 5.

[6] I was hoping to simply make this statement about the ego being the only one of the eight functions that is self-aware, since the logic supporting it is involved. But at least a summary of the logic is owed the reader. A more complete discussion exists in my book *Fundamental Patterns and Functions of Consciousness*. This is an extension of the realizations of Dr. John Lediaev.

Experience involves a subject of an experience, an object experienced, and a process that links the two. When all three (subject, process, and object) are determined, a real experience occurs. Such experiences have a set identity.

It is possible to have configurations of subject, process, and object where one or more of these three values is unspecified. This means that the experience is not rigidly set, but has a range of possibilities for the element(s) that are not unspecified.

The eight fundamental action principles, which I assign to the eight directions embody the eight

References and Notes

possible configurations of subject, process, and object. These can be represented graphically as three lines. The top line is subject, the middle line is process, and the bottom line is object. Each line can be specified (a solid line) or undetermined (a broken line). Thus the following representations: earth — structure and purification (⚏), water — nourishment and connection (☰), fire — transformational change (⚎), air — locational change (⚍), space — perception of value (⚌), mind — coordination (≡), intellect — perception of cause and effect (⚏), and ego — storehouse of impressions (≡). The logic for these relations is beyond the scope of this book, but was worked out in detail by Dr. Lediaev and extended in my thinking.

From these eight graphic representations, it is clear that only ego (≡) is fully determined. Actions and perceptions will conform to the set qualities brought to each situation. The other functions are not so set. They exhibit degrees of freedom in one or more aspects of their structure. Thus, a fully determined awareness only exists for ego, one that exhibits self-sufficiency.

The teaching of verse 6.6 of the *Bhagavad Gītā* is reminiscent of the reality of the operation of ego. It says that, when the self (the ego) is not established in the Self (universal consciousness), universal consciousness behaves as an enemy (the ego is at war with the total situation); when it *is* so established, the universal Self behaves as a friend (the ego's specificity is in the context and has the support of universal law). This means that the 45° rotated swastikas can only be *good*, when they are in the context of enlightened populations, a condition not currently seen in the world.

[7] The two traditional assignments of the *I Ching* trigrams (*Bagua*) to the directions, as used in *Feng Shui,* might yield interesting insights, but, to avoid complications, at this time I have only used the qualities given by the Vedic tradition.

www.ingramcontent.com/pod-product-compliance
Lightning Source LLC
Chambersburg PA
CBHW050024230526
45470CB00003B/1112